JAMIE SMART'S

BUNNY vs MONKEY!

AND THE SUPERSONIC AYE-AYE!

d|b
FICKLING
David Fickling Books

THE PHOENIX

Some of the comics in this book were originally published as
Bunny vs Monkey: The Floating Cow Catastrophe.

Adaptation, additional artwork and colours by Sammy Borras.
Cover design by Paul Duffield and Jamie Smart.

Bunny vs Monkey and the Supersonic Aye-Aye
is A DAVID FICKLING BOOK

First published in Great Britain in 2022 by
David Fickling Books,
31 Beaumont Street,
Oxford,
OX1 2NP

Text and illustrations © Jamie Smart, 2022

978-1-78845-243-4

1 3 5 7 9 10 8 6 4 2

David Fickling Books reg. no. 8340307

A CIP catalogue record for this book is available from the British Library.

Printed by Grafostil, Slovenia.

Papers used by David Fickling Books are from well-managed forests and other responsible sources.

MIX
Paper from
responsible sources
FSC™ C130176

JAMIE SMART'S
BUNNY
VS
MONKEY
AND THE SUPERSONIC AYE-AYE!

"INSOMNIA!"

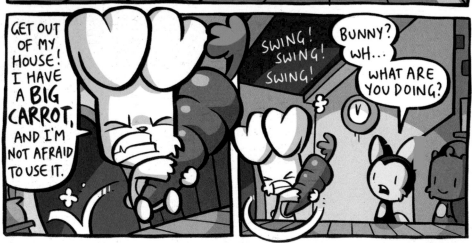

7

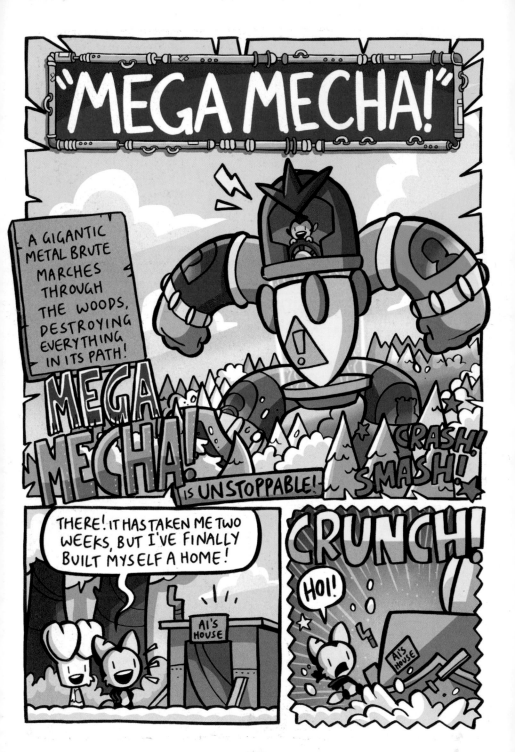

HAR HAR! SKUNKY'S LATEST BRILLIANT INVENTION, MEGA-MECHA, CARES NOT FOR YOUR SILLY LITTLE HOUSE!

BECAUSE I CAME HERE TO DROP THIS BOMB... AND DESTROY EVERYTHING!

DONK DONK!

RUN, AI!

RUN? WHY WOULD I RUN?

IT'S HIM WHO SHOULD BE RUNNING.

HRRRGH!

BLIMEY!

BOING!

SHE'S INSANE!

SHE'S AIMING RIGHT FOR THE BOMB!

11

13

"TAKE TO THE SKIES!"

18

SWOOSH!

THIS IS SUPPOSED TO BE **RELAXING!**

UMM... DOES ANYONE ELSE SEE THAT SHARK?

OH, FOR GOODNESS' SAKE.

THERE'S A **SHARK** IN THE **WHIRLPOOL!**

SHRIEK!

THAT'S JUST MY ROBOT SHARK, **SHARKY.** SOME PEOPLE TAKE A RUBBER DUCK INTO THE BATH, I TAKE A ROBOT SHARK.

BATH? I THOUGHT THIS WAS A TOILET.

RIGHT! THAT'S IT. **OUT,** ALL OF YOU!

22

24

26

27

28

29

PP-WINGGG!

...IS ACTION BEAVER!

CHOO!

WAIT HERE, EVERYONE! I'LL MAKE US ALL BETTER WITH **SCIENCE!**

DOWN IN SKUNKY'S LABORATORY...

WITH JUST ONE STRAND OF ACTION BEAVER'S FUR, I CAN ISOLATE THE PART OF HIS DNA WHICH MAKES HIM IMMUNE TO THIS DASTARDLY COLD!

PLUNK!

FFRP!

I'LL JUST CAREFULLY PLACE THIS INTO THE **SCIENCE-A-TRON...**

AA-CHOO! EURGH!

AND NOW, WE PRESS THE **SCIENCE** BUTTON!

SCIENCE

BOOP!

32

33

BUBBLE TROUBLE!

I HAVE DONE IT!

AFTER WEEKS OF EXPERIMENTING, I HAVE FINALLY CREATED MY **GREATEST INVENTION!**

. . .

WHAT THE WORLD WILL COME TO CALL **SKUNKY'S DOOMSDAY DEVICE!**

WHAT IS IT? CAN I SEE?

ARGH! PIG! GERROFF!

BUMP!

MY **DOOMSDAY DEVICE!**

THP THBTH!

OOPS! BUTTERFINGERS!

WHAT ARE YOU EVEN DOING HERE? THIS IS MY SECRET LABORAT...

VMMMMM!

WHASSAT?

38

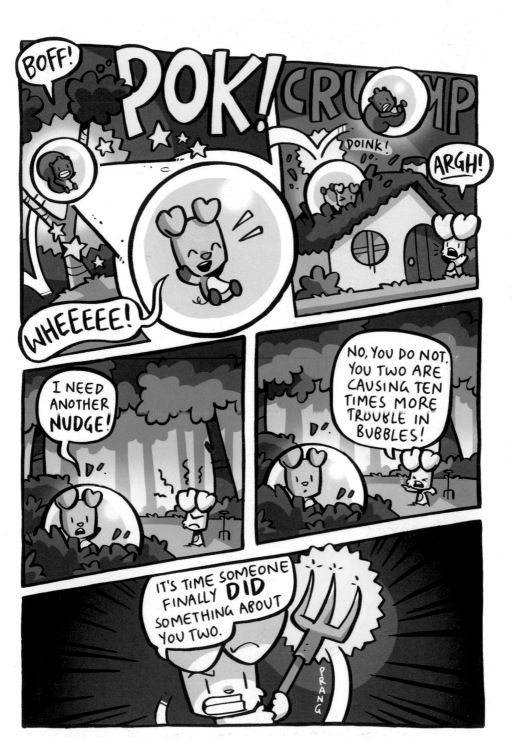

44

"GIANT EGG!"

HAS THERE ALWAYS BEEN A **GIANT EGG** HERE?

HMM, IT'S NOT ON THE MAP.

I'LL BET IT'S ONE OF SKUNKY'S EXPERIMENTS! ANOTHER DEVIOUS SCHEME TO HELP HIM DESTROY THE WORLD.

BEEP BOOP BEEP!

IN SKUNKY'S LAIR...

BRING! BRING!

YYY-ELLO?

WE FOUND YOUR GIANT EGG!

SORRY, WHO IS THIS?

IT'S, UH... **BUNNY!** WE FOUND YOUR EGG! WHAT'S IN IT?

OH C'MON! I CAN'T BE EXPECTED TO REMEMBER **EVERY** HEINOUS EXPERIMENT I COME UP WITH.

EVIL PLANS

EGG.

EGG EGG.

ARE YOU SURE IT'S MINE?

WELL, IT'S NOT MINE.

WE'RE JUST LUCKY IT HASN'T CRACKED OPEN YET. IF IT IS SOMETHING I DESIGNED, WHAT'S INSIDE COULD BE ABSOLUTELY HORRIFIC!

CRAAACK!

UM.

WHAT DO WE DO, SKUNKY? WHAT DO WE **DOOOOO?**

YOU HAVE TO GET RID OF THE EGG! BEFORE IT'S TOO LATE!

AND **HOW** ARE WE SUPPOSED TO GET **RID** OF IT?!

HEAVE!!

I HAVE AN IDEA!

IT'S BREAKING APART! WE'RE DOOMED!

I CAN SEE A CLEARING! WE CAN LEAVE IT...

...HERE.

OH.

SPLOSH!

WE DID IT, SKUNKY! WE SET YOUR EXPERIMENT FREE!

THAT'S ALL WELL AND GOOD, BUT...

IN MY EXPERIENCE, IT'S NOT USUALLY THE **EGG** YOU HAVE TO WORRY ABOUT.

LIKE WHAT? I ONLY KNOW HOW TO EAT ANTS!

BOO HOO HOO... GASP! I'VE HAD AN IDEA!

I'M THE BEST COOK IN THE WHOLE WOODS! I'LL **TEACH** YOU HOW TO MAKE DELICIOUS, ANT-FREE MEALS!

OKAY!

UP IN WEENIE'S HOUSE...

...SO THEN YOU FOLD THE EGGS AND SUGAR INTO THE BATTER...

UM...WHAT EGGS?

THE EGGS I GAVE YOU!

WHAT HAPPENED TO THE EGGS I GAVE YOU?

OH, I THOUGHT THOSE WERE FOR THROWING AT **MONKEY**.

WHATEVER THIS GAME IS, I'M NOT PLAYING.

HUFF!

OH, I GIVE UP! YOU THREW AWAY MY EGGS, YOU PUT CUSTARD IN MY OVEN, AND THE ONLY THING YOU'VE MADE IS **THIS**.

I THOUGHT THAT WAS QUITE GOOD.

55

56

To take his mind off the multiple BEE-STINGS, Bunny decided to go for a walk...

MY POOR BOOK! I'LL NEVER FINISH IT AT THIS RATE.

CHOMP!

RRRRRRR!

SORRY, HE'S A BIT 'BITEY' TODAY!

NOOOO!

THIS IS MY BOOK! MY NOVEL ABOUT LIFE IN THE WOODS! AND YOU'VE ALL RUINED IT!

A NOVEL?

CAN WE READ IT?

And so, because all his friends were really stupid, Bunny gave up on writing and barricaded himself in his house instead.

OOOH!

I WONDER IF IT'S BASED ON ANYONE WE KNOW?

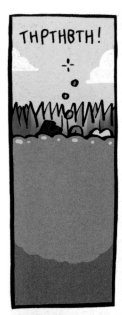

CALM DOWN, PIG. THERE'S NO SUCH THING AS ALIENS.

PROVE IT!

FINE. I WILL. BUT WE'LL NEED A PLAN.

ARE YOU **SURE** THIS IS THE RIGHT WAY, PIG?

I CAN'T SEE!

I'M A COW'S BOTTOM!

KEEP GOING!

CAN WE STOP A MINUTE? THIS PANTOMIME COW SMELLS LIKE PANTS.

CHUNK!

HELLO?

71

HA HA HA! YOU LOOK RIDICULOUS!

MONKEY! SKUNKY! SO YOU'VE BEEN STEALING THE COWS!

OF COURSE!

HOW ELSE WOULD WE MAKE MILKSHAKES?

WE DO NEED A LOT OF MILK.

W...WHY ARE YOU MAKING MILKSHAKES?

73

"SCREWBALL 4000!"

76

HELLO, BUNNY! WE COULDN'T FIND A 'VEHICLE', SO I'M JUST PUSHING PIG AROUND IN A **BIN!**

CRASH!

BUNNY 1

NOOOO! I'M SO CLOSE TO THE FINISH LINE!

IF I LOSE THE RACE, I'LL LOSE MY BET WITH MONKEY, AND...

FINISH

SWAMP!

HANG ON...

...WHERE IS MONKEY?

FINISH

SWAMP

80

Then Stinky Monkey OVERLOADED the bogey gun...

click click click!

cool

...and it fired out the BIGGEST BOGEY in the ENTIRE UNIVERSE!!

Bloorp!

Hur!

THERE'S TOO MUCH ABOUT BOGEYS NOW. I WANT TO MAKE IT ABOUT ME BEING QUEEN AGAIN.

NO, NO, WAIT! THIS IS BRILLIANT!

Then Stinky Monkey ROLLED the giant bogey down the hill, before FLICKING it at BUNNY'S HOUSE!

Flickk!

"BLEURGHH!" Bunny said, like an idiot. Blugh! Eugh! GROSSSSS! Ha ha!

Bleurgh!

Ha ha!

86

89

92

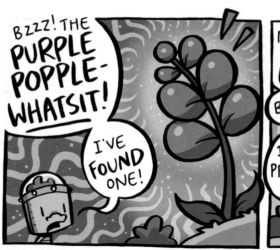

BZZZ! THE **PURPLE POPPLEWHATSIT!**

I'VE FOUND ONE!

MOST **RARE** OF ALL FLOWERS. MOST **EXQUISITE!**

BZZ.

I WILL PROTECT YOU.

OOOH, IS THAT A **PURPLE POPPLEWHATSIT?**

BZZ. HUH?

I'VE HEARD THAT THESE ARE RATHER DELICIOUS WHEN COOKED IN AUBERGINE STEW.

BZZT! NO!

NO ONE MUST TOUCH THE **PURPLE POPPLEWHATSIT!**

SCREAM!

BZZ ZAP!

IS **THAT** WHAT THAT FLOWER IS? PERHAPS I COULD SYNTHESISE IT INTO SOME SORT OF **PURPLE SERUM...**

...AND COVER THE WOODS IN A BRIGHT **PURPLE GOO!**

SKUNKY'S FINEST INVENTION YET!

YOU KNOW HOW I LIKE TO BE INSPIRED BY WILDLIFE, TO BASE MY TERRIFYING CREATIONS ON THE ANIMAL KINGDOM?

TO REPLICATE THEIR ABILITIES DOWN TO THE FINEST DETAIL...

...WELL, THIS WALRUS FIRES ROCKETS OUT ITS NOSE!

FOOSH!

HAR HAR!

ONWARD, WALRUS! NUKE NATURE WITH YOUR NASAL NAPALM!

LOLLOP! LOLLOP! LOLLOP!

BOOM!

AIIEE!

BOOM!

THAT'S QUITE FAR ENOUGH!

"SUN KINDA TROUBLE!"

ANYONE ELSE GETTING TOO HOT?

NOPE.

IT'S WEIRD—WE'RE IN THE SHADE, BUT IT'S GETTING REALLY TOASTY.

IT'S NICE AND COOL UP IN THE TREES.

AIIIEE! MY SUN-LOUNGER IS CATCHING FIRE!

FWOOM!

107

109

I'LL HOLD THEM BACK WITH THIS SHRUB! YOU TWO RUN FOR YOUR LIVES!

OH.

THEY'VE GONE.

MAYBE I'M GOING TO NEED MORE THAN STICKS TO BRING DOWN A DRAGON, ANYWAY.

BURNT!

WEENIE!

I'M HIDING! BOO HOO HOO! YOU CAN'T SEE ME!

I NEED ALL YOUR POTS, PANS AND BAKING TRAYS!

OOH! ARE WE GOING TO MAKE A CAKE?

EVEN BETTER...

I'VE BEEN LIVING THIS SAME DAY **OVER AND OVER!**

I FOUND YOUR NEW **POCKET-SIZED TIME TRAVEL DEVICE** AND DECIDED TO EAT IT!

DON'T ASK ME WHY, I'M A MONKEY.

IT DID SOMETHING TO ME. NOW I'M CURSED TO WAKE UP EVERY MORNING AND LIVE THROUGH **THE EXACT SAME DAY.**

I KNOW EVERYTHING THAT'S GOING TO HAPPEN.

FOR EXAMPLE, I KNOW PIG'S GOING TO BE CHASED BY BEES.

WORST BIRTHDAY EVER!

BZzzz

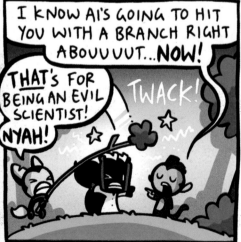

I KNOW AI'S GOING TO HIT YOU WITH A BRANCH RIGHT ABOUUUUT...**NOW!**

THAT'S FOR BEING AN EVIL SCIENTIST! NYAH!

TWACK!

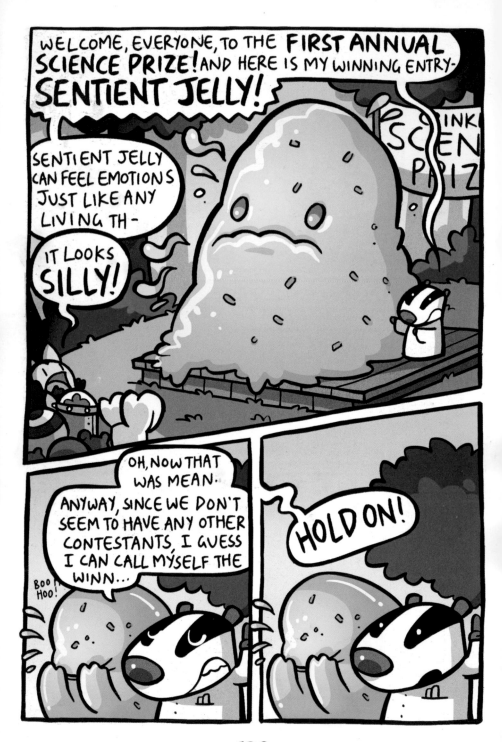

120

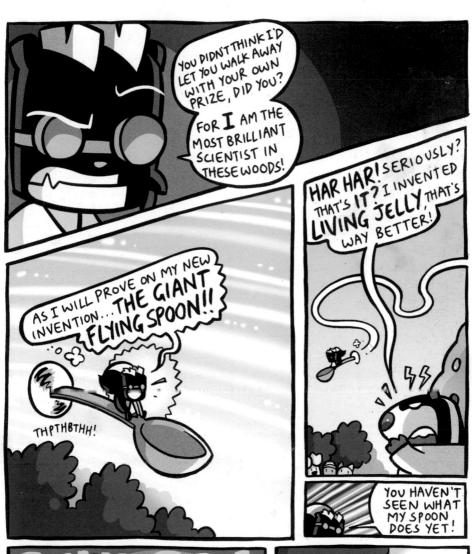

(DEREK THE SENTIENT JELLY WAS RESHAPED AND NOW LIVES A VERY HAPPY LIFE AS A BOUNCY CASTLE)

"EVIL BUNNY!"

TUESDAY, AND THE WOODLAND ANIMALS ARE BATTLING SKUNKY'S LATEST INVENTION.

SPIDER CHOPS!

BLAHH!

YAHH!

HRRG!

IF I CAN JUST GET THE MAIN CONTROL PANEL LOOSE, I MIGHT BE ABLE TO SHORT CIRCUIT IT...

MAIN CONTROL PANEL

AHA!

HERE I COME TO HELP, BUNNY! WITH MY WEAPON OF CHOICE...

...A SAUCEPAN!

126

"THE BRAVEST SQUIRREL IN THE WOODS!"

IT'S - PUFF - NO USE. I CAN'T - PUFF - DO IT, I CAN'T BE - PUFF - BRAVE!

OOH, I'M GOING TO BE SICK.

NONSENSE! YOU HIRED ME, SKUNKY, MASTER OF THE MACABRE, TO **CURE** YOUR FEAR! TO HELP YOU FIND ~YOUR~ **INNER HERO!!**

AND THAT'S WHAT I INTEND TO D...

GET OUT FROM BEHIND ME!

I CAN'T! I'M WETTING MYSELF!

HMM, PERHAPS SENDING YOU OUT INTO THE DARK WASN'T ENOUGH.

PERHAPS YOU NEED SOMETHING TO **REALLY** BE SCARED OF...

129

130

134

135

NO, OF COURSE YOU DIDN'T. YOU'RE JUST A BUNNY RABBIT.

HOW SILLY OF ME.

HEH.

RIGHT, HE'S LOOKING THE OTHER WAY. NOW'S YOUR CHANCE!

RUN AWAY!

BUT HE WANTED TO KNOW WHAT CAUSED ALL THIS TROUBLE!!

FWOOM FWOOM! FWOOM!

SO LEMME SHOW HIM MY METEORITE CANNON!!

NO, SKUNKY! NOOO!

CLONK! CLONK!

OW! OW!!

BZZZZZZZ

IT'S VITALLY IMPORTANT HE STAYS ALIVE!

I JUST WANTED TO SHOW OFF.

BOOM!!

AHA! I FOUND A CHOCOLATE BAR FOR YOU, LITTLE...

...SKUNK?!

WHERE DID YOU COME FROM?

PAF!

AND HOW DID THE LITTLE BUNNY GET BEHIND ME?

UMM...

141

WE THINK YOU WORK TOO HARD SO WE BAKED YOU SOME **DOUGHNUTS.**

HELLO?

HELLOOO?

QUIET, SIMPLETON! I HAVE JUST SYNTHESISED MY GREATEST CREATION YET!

PSCHH!

THE **MULTIPLYER!!** JUST ONE DROP OF THIS LIQUID WILL MAKE **EXACT COPIES** OF ANY OBJECT IT TOUCHES!

SO...I'M GOING TO POUR IT ALL OVER **MYSELF!**

144

I CREATE THESE INCREDIBLE MACHINES. **BEAUTIFUL** MACHINES. WAY BEYOND WHAT A SKUNK SHOULD REALISTICALLY BE ABLE TO CREATE!

AND HOW DOES EVERYONE RESPOND?

THEY **RUN AWAY! SCREAMING!**

FLAPPING THEIR ARMS, LIKE THIS.

EEK! EEK! EEK!

PERHAPS ALWAYS TRYING TO DESTROY EVERYTHING ISN'T THE BEST WAY TO BE APPRECIATED.

WHAT'S THAT, DESTRUCTOTRON 3000?

YOU'RE RIGHT! THE WORLD **IS** RICH WITH BEAUTY, AND **FILLED** WITH EXPERIENCES.

I **SHOULD** GIVE UP ON EVIL SCIENCE, AND BASK IN THE GLORY OF LIFE!

JUST LIKE YOU SAID.

AHHH.

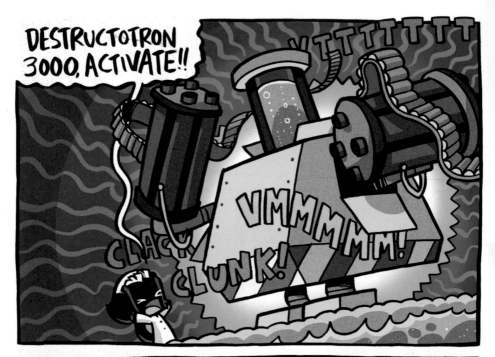

FOR TOO LONG, BUNNY AND HIS IDIOT FRIENDS HAVE RULED OVER THESE WOODS.

SO IT IS TIME WE BAND TOGETHER, EACH OF US USING OUR UNIQUE SKILLS, TO **CONQUER!**

ACTION BEAVER'S FARTING, AND IT SMELLS LIKE **GOOSEBERRIES!**

GOOD. THEN THAT IS HIS **UNIQUE SKILL!**

FRRPP!

JUST AS **METAL STEVE'S** UNIQUE SKILL IS HIS LOVE OF **DESTRUCTION!**

DESTROY!

AND **SKUNKY,** YOUR UNIQUE SKILL IS YOUR INCREDIBLE **INVENTING BRAIN!**

I'VE CREATED A RAYGUN THAT TURNS THINGS INTO **CUSTARD!**

WELL, I'M SURE THAT'LL BE USEFUL SOMEHOW.

WHAT'S **YOUR** UNIQUE SKILL, COMMANDER MONKEY?

155

156

'WILL-O'-DE-WISP!'

160

161

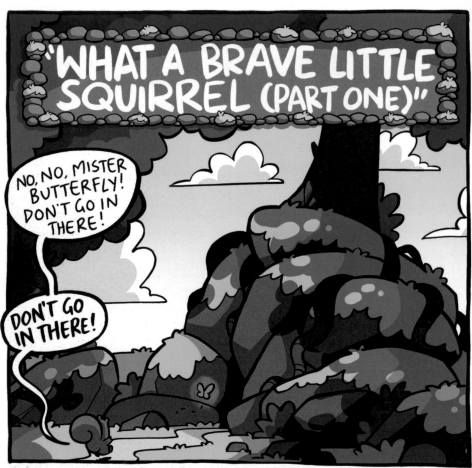

165

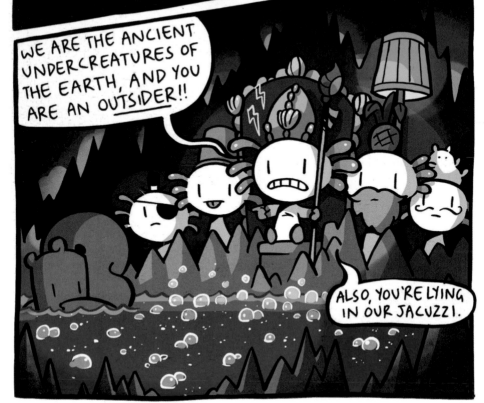

168

SECRET SCIENCE STUFF. YOU WOULDN'T UNDERSTAND.

NO OKAY, I JUST FILLED SOME JARS WITH **BEES** AND STUCK THEM TO THE BOTTOM OF A PIECE OF WOOD.

BZZ! BZZ! BZZ! BZZ!

GENETICALLY MODIFIED **SUPER** BEES, GRANTED. BUT ALL YOU NEED TO KNOW IS THAT IT <u>WORKS</u>!

THAT, AND...

...IT'S YOURS TO BUY FOR ONLY **NINE NINETY-NINE!** STOCKS ARE LIMITED!! GET YOURS NOW!

ME! ME! OOH!

HOVERBOARD

A1? YOU'RE THE ONLY ONE WITHOUT A HOVERBOARD.

HOVERBOA

PAH! I DON'T FOLLOW TRENDS.

MEH, SHAME. DOESN'T BOTHER ME THOUGH, I'VE MADE ENOUGH MONEY TO BUY WHAT I'VE ALWAYS WANTED...

173

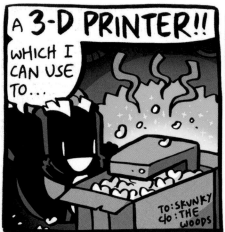

A 3-D PRINTER!! WHICH I CAN USE TO...

TO: SKUNKY c/o: THE WOODS

MAKE TOYS OF MYSELF, WHICH I WILL THEN SELL ALONGSIDE...

BEEP! BOOP!

BEEPY BEEP BOOP!

...THE REST OF MY **SKUNKY MERCHANDISING RANGE!**

GOOD AT BEING EVIL

SKUNKY SAYS RELAX!

TOYS!

MUGS

MERCHANDISING IS WHERE THE REAL MONEY IS. IF I CAN MAKE MYSELF INTO A POPULAR BRAND, I'LL BE... **FILTHY RICH!**

SKUNKY

SOME TIME LATER...

POO.

NOT ONE SALE.

IT'S SKUNKY!

175

176

177

180

182

EVERY WEEK, SOME NEW THREAT BEFALLS US ALL. WHETHER IT'S SKUNKY NEARLY DESTROYING THE WORLD, SWARMS OF BEES, HUGE DOUGHNUTS, HUMANS, MANIACAL BADGERS...

BOOM! BOOM! BOOM!

AND EVERY TIME, WE DEFEAT THEM. BUT FOR HOW LONG? IT'S THE LAW OF AVERAGES THAT ONE DAY SOMETHING IS GOING TO BREAK THROUGH...

...AND BEAT US!

YOU'RE BEING PARANOID!

I'M BEING PREPARED!

NOTHING'S GOING TO GET ME UP HERE!

DID YOU HEAR THAT, MONKEY? APPARENTLY SOME SORT OF GRAVE DANGER IS COMING TO THE WOODS.

THAT'S MY FAVOURITE KIND OF DANGER!

"THE OTHER SIDE!"

OHHH I LOVE TO COOK...

...I COOK ALL DAY...

...COOKING SENDS...

...ALL THE BAD THOUGHTS AWAY...

THERE REALLY ARE SO MANY WAYS YOU COULD IMPROVE YOUR COOKING!

I... WHAT?

NO THERE AREN'T!

YOU CAN RELY ON US, ONCE AGAIN, TO TURN YOU INTO A **MASTER CHEF!**

WHERE ARE YOU?

WHY ARE YOU SAYING THESE THINGS?

ARE YOU BEHIND THESE BOXES?

WELCOME BACK!

AIEE!

HERE ON **FOODIE T.V.**, WE HAVE SOMETHING TO MAKE COOKERY SO MUCH EASIER!

MY OLD TV?

I DIDN'T THINK IT WORKED!

THE **MULTI-KITCHEN BUDDY!!**

IT BAKES!

IT GLAZES!

IT POACHES!

IT BROILS!

IT REALLY IS A MIRACLE! A MULTI-PURPOSE KITCHEN UTENSIL! EVERYONE HAS ONE!

DO YOU?

189

NO MATTER, IT WON'T SURVIVE OUR SECOND WAVE OF WOODLAND DEFENCE...

KAKAPO BIRDS... POOP!!

THRPP!

THRP!

?!

THAT'S MORE OF AN INCONVENIENCE THAN A HARDENED DEFENCE, ISN'T IT?

JUST WAIT. KAKAPO POOP IS QUITE UNIQUE. WHEN IT BUILDS UP, IT...

EXPLODES!

BOOM!

BOOM!

'ELLO, WHAT DO WE HAVE HERE?

NEXT LINE OF DEFENCE - UGLY WARTHOGS!

NOW HANG ON, WE AGREED TO HELP OUT, BUT NO ONE SAID ANYTHING ABOUT NAME CALLING.

IT'S GETTING AWAY!

WHEEZE! WHEEZE!

193

"RUNNNN!"

THEY SAY YOU'RE THE FASTEST CREATURE IN THESE WOODS.

YOU DON'T LOOK VERY FAST.

SLURRRP!

IT'S MY DAY OFF.

YOU'RE NOT PANICKING ABOUT THIS 'GRAVE DANGER' ON ITS WAY TO THE WOODS?

NAH, I CAN HANDLE ANYTHING.

OR OUTRUN IT.

I DON'T BELIEVE YOU'RE VERY FAST AT ALL. IF YOU WERE, YOU'D PROVE IT.

NOPE. DON'T HAVE TO.

SPLOSH!!

ACK!

BIBBLE!

NOT THIS AGAIN, ACTION BEAVER!

196

197

"THE WORST IDEA YOU'VE EVER HAD!"

DO YOU KNOW WHAT THAT IS, MONKEY?

IS IT A JELLY WORM?

A LIME-FLAVOURED JELLY WORM?

NO, YOU IDIOT. IT'S A **CATERPILLAR!** ONE OF NATURE'S MOST INCREDIBLE INSECTS. DO YOU KNOW WHY?

IT TASTES LIKE LIME?

NO! IT FORMS A **COCOON!** AND IT STAYS IN THAT COCOON UNTIL IT EMERGES AS A **BUTTERFLY!**

COCOON!

LUCKY I BROUGHT THIS FLIP-CHART WITH ME.

AND IT IS THE **COCOON** WHICH HAS INSPIRED THE BEST IDEA I'VE EVER HAD!

WHAT DOES IT DOOOO?

EVERYONE IN THESE WOODS IS SCARED OF SOMETHING COMING TO GET US. WHATEVER FORCE OR BEAST THAT MIGHT BE.

BUT ME, I DON'T KNOW FEAR. I ONLY KNOW SCIENCE!! I WANT TO CAPTURE THIS THING!

I WILL LURE IT INTO THE MAIN CHAMBER BY LEAVING A DELICIOUS BANANA AS BAIT...

AHEM.

HELLO.

GET **OUT** OF THE **COCOONINATOR** YOU GREEDY PIG!

BUT I HAVEN'T HAD BREAKFAST.

BOOT!

AHEM! I WILL LURE IT INTO THE MAIN CHAMBER BY LEAVING **ANOTHER** DELICIOUS BANANA AS BAIT.

AND THEN THE COCOONINATOR FILLS WITH A GELATINOUS LIQUID HARVESTED FROM CATERPILLARS, WHICH WILL FREEZE THE BEAST—**WHAT ARE YOU DOING?**

WHAT?

THIS MACHINE COULD FREEZE YOU IN STASIS, FOREVER!

WELL STOP LEAVING DELICIOUS BANANAS IN IT THEN!

EVIL PLOT EVILLY PLOTTING.

YOU KNOW WHAT? FINE. HERE, HAVE MORE BANANAS. HAVE **LOADS** OF BANANAS!

CHUCK!

YAY!

BECAUSE A **PIG** WILL BE FAR TASTIER BAIT TO A **MONSTER! MWAH HA!**

HAR HAR!

MWOO HAR!

CHOMP CHOMP

WHAT'S THAT SMALLER CHAMBER FOR?

OH, THAT'S TO CAPTURE GHOSTS. IN CASE THE MONSTER IS A GHOST.

G-G-GHOST? NO WAY AM I EATING BANANAS NEXT TO A GHOST!

EEEE!

HEY! COME BACK!

BAH! I WAS FOOLISH TO THINK PIG WOULD BE STUPID ENOUGH TO STICK AROUND.

HEY, WHY'VE YOU STOPPED THROWING BANANAS IN?

MORE BANANAS!

203

206

208

210

RIGHT, THIS HAS GOT OUT OF HAND NOW. SKUNKY, LET US BACK OUT.

UMM...

THE COCOONINATOR CAN'T BE CONTROLLED FROM THE INSIDE. WE'RE **LOCKED** IN HERE.

AND THE CONTROL PANEL IS OUT THERE.

DOOR START

HOW TO DRAW ★AI★

①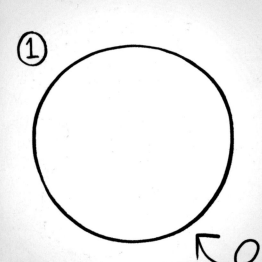

AI MAY BE A NEW CHARACTER IN THE WOODS, BUT SHE'S DRAWN IN A SIMILAR WAY TO MONKEY AND ACTION BEAVER. SO WE START BY DRAWING A **CIRCLE** FOR HER **HEAD!**

②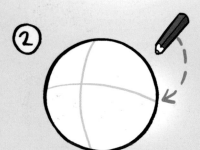

DRAWING A CROSS LIKE THIS HELPS US TO WORK OUT WHERE HER FACE SHOULD GO.

③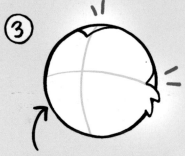

BUT BEFORE AI'S FACE, WE NEED TO DRAW THE OUTLINE OF HER **FUR**... LIKE THIS!

④

THEN **EARS!** AI'S EARS LOOK LIKE TRIANGLES WITH CURVED SIDES.

⑤

PUT TWO EARS ON HER HEAD, BUT DON'T FORGET THE EAR ON THE LEFT HAS A SLIGHT TEAR IN IT!

⑥

NOW, AI'S **FACE!** WE ALWAYS START WITH TWO LINES FOR THE EYES...

⑦

...WITH A COUPLE OF EYEBROWS...

⑧

...A LITTLE TRIANGLE FOR HER **NOSE**...

⑨

...AND LET'S ADD A WIDE **SMILING MOUTH!**

FINALLY, WE NEED TO DRAW AI'S **BODY!**

①

LET'S DRAW AI DOING HER FAVOURITE THING, **RUNNING!!** HER BODY IS A LUMP SHAPE, BUT IT CURVES A LITTLE, AS IF IT'S BEING PULLED ALONG BY HER HEAD!

②

③

LET'S HAVE ONE ARM REACHING OUT IN FRONT OF AI. WE'RE GOING TO CHEAT A BIT HERE... IT WOULDN'T REALLY STRETCH THIS FAR FROM HER BODY, BUT WE CAN JUST TUCK IT BEHIND HER HEAD!

FOR **FEET**, WE ONLY NEED TO DRAW CIRCLES. ONE IN FRONT, ONE TUCKED BEHIND!

④

HER OTHER ARM TRAILS OUT BEHIND HER...

⑤ ADD A BUSHY TAIL, AND SHE'S **DONE!** A DYNAMIC PICTURE OF AI, SPEEDING FORWARDS TO SAVE THE DAY!

①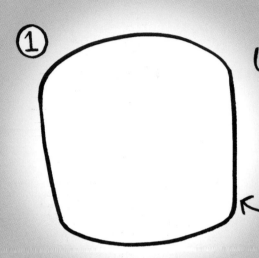

WEENIE's HEAD SHAPE IS MORE SIMILAR TO BUNNY AND PIG'S... IT'S LIKE A SQUARE, BUT A **BULGING SQUARE!**

②

AS EVER, IT HELPS TO PENCIL IN A CROSS TO HELP US WORK OUT WHERE TO PUT A FACE.

③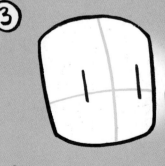

AND WITH JUST A COUPLE OF LINES, WEENIE HAS **EYES!**

④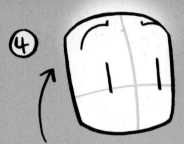

TWO MORE LINES FOR **EYEBROWS**. WEENIE IS OFTEN EITHER HAPPY OR SHOCKED... BUT RAISED EYEBROWS WORK FOR **BOTH** OF THESE EXPRESSIONS!

⑤

A LITTLE TRIANGLE FOR A **NOSE**...

⑥

AND A SMALL CURVED LINE FOR A SWEET **SMILE!**

⑦

LET'S NOT FORGET THE LITTLE TUFT OF FUR FOR A **CHEEK!**

⑧

EARS! WEENIE'S EARS ARE LITTLE LUMPS ON EITHER SIDE OF THE HEAD.

⑨

AND LASTLY, ADD A SWIRL FOR A **QUIFF OF HAIR!**

①

LIKE ALL THE CHARACTERS IN BUNNY VS MONKEY, WEENIE'S BODY IS A CURVED LUMP!

②

HERE, WE'RE GOING TO DRAW WEENIE HOLDING SOME FOOD! SO LET'S HAVE AN ARM STRETCHED OUT WITH AN OVEN GLOVE ON IT!

③

THAT ARM IS HOLDING A DISH, WHICH IS LIKE A SQUASHED CIRCLE.

④

POP A CUPCAKE ON TOP OF IT. COPY THIS ONE, OR MAKE UP YOUR OWN!

⑤ ADD A TAIL! A BIG BUSHY TAIL BULGING OUT FROM BEHIND!

AND WE'VE DRAWN WEENIE, HOLDING A DELICIOUS CUPCAKE!

TRY DRAWING ALL SORTS OF WEIRD AND WONDERFUL FOOD ON THE DISH!

COMING SOON

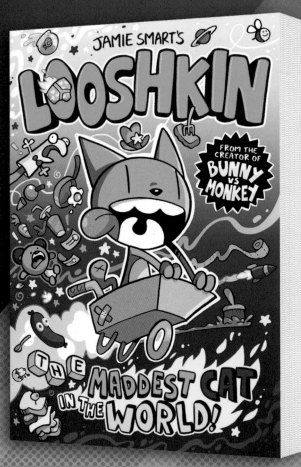

AND NOW, A SNEAK PEEK INTO THE WILD WORLD OF LOOSHKIN...

ONCE UPON A TIME, A LITTER OF KITTENS WAS BORN. THEY WERE BEAUTIFUL AND CUTE AND EVERYONE WANTED TO OWN ONE OF THEM...

WELL, ALL EXCEPT ONE THEY HID OUT THE BACK...

ARE YOU SURE YOU WANT 'IM? 'E JUST AIN'T RIGHT.

STORE

THINGS GO...WRONG AROUND 'IM.

WELL, HE'S THE ONLY ONE LEFT.

BONK! SQUEAK! BONK!

WHAT'S HIS NAME?

BUM!

BOSH!

LOOSHKIN

AND SO BEGINS
OUR TALE OF...

...THE MADDEST CAT
IN THE WORLD.

FART!

FFRP!

IN THE BACK GARDEN...

LADY LOOSHKIN OF LOOSHIRE, IT IS MOST WONDERFUL OF YOU TO JOIN OUR GARDEN TEA PARTY.

I EVEN BAKED A CAKE, TO CELEBRATE!

OH NO, I FORGOT THE CLOUDY LEMONADE! WHAT A BAD HOST YOU MUST THINK ME.

WAIT THERE! I'LL BE RIGHT BACK!

MEANWHILE, INSIDE LOOSHKIN'S MIND...

SCREEE-EEAM!!

HELP US! SHE'S QUITE MAD!

227

230

ENTER THE WORLD OF
JAMIE SMART'S

FLEMBER

**DISCOVER THE MAGICAL
POWER OF FLEMBER, WITH
BOY-INVENTOR DEV, AND HIS
BEST FRIEND BOJA
THE BEAR!**

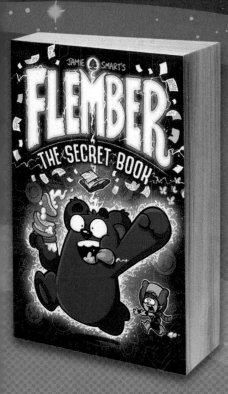

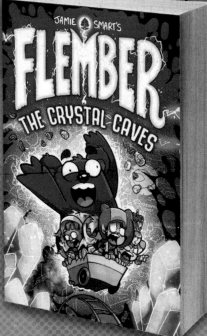

THERE ARE MANY MORE HILARIOUS HIJINKS IN THESE OTHER ASTONISHING

BUNNY VS MONKEY

BOOKS!

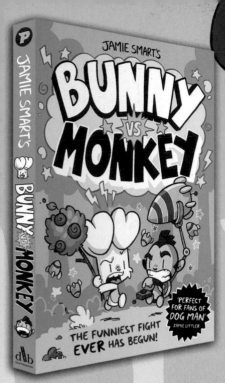

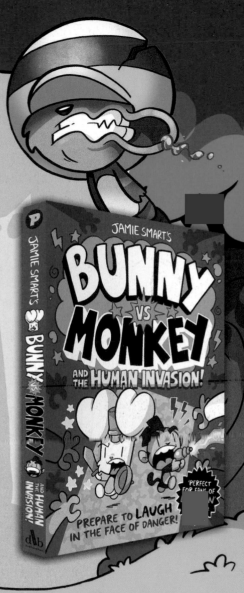

WITH
MANY MORE
COMING
SOON!

JAMIE SMART

PHOTO BY STEVE BROWN

HAHAHA!

JAMIE SMART HAS BEEN CREATING CHILDREN'S COMICS FOR MANY YEARS, WITH POPULAR TITLES INCLUDING *BUNNY VS MONKEY*, *LOOSHKIN* AND *FISH-HEAD STEVE*, WHICH BECAME THE FIRST WORK OF ITS KIND TO BE SHORTLISTED FOR THE ROALD DAHL FUNNY PRIZE.

THE FIRST THREE BOOKS IN HIS *FLEMBER* SERIES OF ILLUSTRATED NOVELS ARE AVAILABLE NOW. HE ALSO WORKS ON MULTIMEDIA PROJECTS LIKE *FIND CHAFFY*.

JAMIE LIVES IN THE SOUTH-EAST OF ENGLAND, WHERE HE SPENDS HIS TIME THINKING UP STORIES AND GETTING LOST ON DOG WALKS.